LIFE & LEGACY OF A
VOLUNTEER

True Tales of Teamwork, Trials, and Triumphs leading to Real Change

KEN HOYLE

Life & Legacy of a Volunteer
Copyright © 2023 by Ken Hoyle

All rights reserved. No part of this publication may be reproduced, distributed, or transmitted in any form or by any means, including photocopying, recording, or other electronic or mechanical methods, without the prior written permission of the author, except in the case of brief quotations embodied in critical reviews and certain other non-commercial uses permitted by copyright law.

Tellwell Talent
www.tellwell.ca

ISBN
978-0-2288-9577-0 (Paperback)
978-0-2288-9578-7 (eBook)

Table of Contents

If I knew then... 1

1. Curtain Call 5
2. Campaign Promises 11
3. The art of quitting 17
4. Luck on a bus 20
5. Margaret the Bulldog 23
6. Rotary Forest and Rotary Food 29
7. Elephants on Main Street 33
8. The grit to say No 36
9. Newfoundland hospitality 40
10. How to hoist a train station 43
11. How to revive a dying tree 50
12. Six parking spaces 53
13. What a difference a name makes 57
14. Mad as hell and doomed to fail 59
15. The joy of volunteering 63
16. Leadership at its best 67
17. Fighting fires, fighting sabotage 71
18. What "okay" really means 78
19. The importance of a badge 82
20. Village coup d'etat 84

What a ride! 87
Acknowledgments 95
About The Author 96

If I knew then...

Over sixty years ago, at the age of eleven, I began volunteering. As you might expect, I was eager, naïve, and in for a heap of learning. I soldiered on, stumbling through challenges, upsets, hard work, disillusionment, and disappointments to capture unforgettable victories.

Today, I continue volunteering, equipped with a lifetime of learning. And I want to share my learning with you.

In fact, this book is yet another volunteer experience. I am hoping to help both volunteers and organizations by sharing 20 stories from my experiences with both local and national organizations.

I want the main message to be clear from cover to cover: the giving must be mutual. As a volunteer, if you give more than you receive in any project or role, you risk getting sucked into what I call the Volunteer Vortex. Your health and the success of the project can both suffer. As an organization, if you demand or expect more from your volunteers than you are willing to give them, your volunteers will become a liability rather than an asset, and you will face recurring losses both in human resources and expenses.

It's as simple as that.

Volunteers contribute to the economic vitality of a community, building and strengthening civic pride. They come from all walks of life, adding diversity, knowledge, wisdom, and enthusiasm to a community, helping it change over time to meet new challenges. Volunteers also help businesses succeed, for short-term projects and emergencies, and over the long term on committees.

As many studies have shown, volunteering can be good for your mental health, and it certainly has been for mine. Along with a rewarding career as a Landscape Architect, volunteering has enabled me to focus on matters other than my own. It has helped give me purpose and has vastly enriched my life.

However, it is also true that volunteers burn out, get disillusioned, and feel unappreciated. If they don't quit in frustration and anger, they may carry on while purposefully undermining the organization. Other volunteers allow their dedication to run their lives, losing life balance and sacrificing self-care in favour of their organization. In some cases, a volunteer is assigned a task doomed to failure because it should be assigned to a paid professional.

Organizations lose out, wasting countless hours recruiting and training new volunteers, perpetuating the cycle of burnout and high turnover.

How do you break this cycle? The giving must be mutual.

I have learned this important lesson while working both as a volunteer and as a manager of volunteers.

VOLUNTEERS:

Read my stories to learn how to avoid pitfalls and make your experiences more rewarding. As you gain experience, you will become increasingly valuable to your current organization and future ones. Through exposure to new environments, you can stretch your comfort zone, make new friends, connect with potential employers, and acquire a wealth of knowledge.

Most importantly, you can discover ways to derive the greatest satisfaction from your volunteering and avoid falling victim to burnout or disillusionment. It's all about balance and mental health.

ORGANIZATIONS:

Read my stories to learn how to effectively manage your volunteers and maximize their productivity and longevity. Whether you are a community organization, government agency, charity, small business, or corporation, you can glean insights from my stories on how to help you and your volunteers thrive.

In chronological order, these vivid snippets remain etched in my memory, replete with humour, heartbreak, and pride. Enjoy.

1. Curtain Call

Stage Crew, School Play, Norseman Public School, Etobicoke, Ontario 1960 (age 11)

Act I of my volunteer career opened when I was eleven years old – you know, that age where you want to contribute to your community, enhance your local culture, and make the world a better place.

Well, not exactly. I just wanted to skip class.

It's not that I didn't enjoy school. During the mornings, my 6th Grade teacher would find me sitting quietly at my desk, writing copious notes, and occasionally raising my hand to ask serious questions. But there's only so long a growing boy can stay confined to the same desk in the same room. I yearned to run outside in the sun, chase my buddy Harry to the fence, throw a football, and catch a frog.

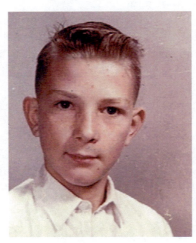

And so, by early afternoon, restlessness took hold. Nouns, verbs, integers, and historic battles were replaced by spitballs, flying rubber bands, giggles, and snorts.

"Hoyle, Robertson: OUT." The teacher pointed to the door.

My friend Harry and I were promptly banished to sit on the cold, unforgiving floors of the hallway, subjected to even greater boredom than the Seven Years War.

However, boredom can serve as fertile soil for a curious mind.

"Hey Harry! Look!" I pointed across the hall.

"Huh? What?"

VOLUNTEERS WANTED, the poster said. PIED PIPER, SCHOOL PLAY. SEE MR. FILMON.

Harry was not interested.

"But Harry, think of it," I whispered. "Volunteers get out of class for rehearsals."

"So you're going to be a movie star?"

I didn't know for sure. But as soon as school finished for the day I knocked on Mr. Filmon's door. He shook my hand and escorted me to the stage.

"The story is called Pied Piper. Do you want to audition for a part?"

"That sounds too scary."

"How about costumes? Do you have a sewing machine?"

Both of us laughed.

"Okay, Ken, maybe you could help out back-stage. How would you like to be the curtain caller?"

Now that sounded good. It made me feel important. I would pull a rope to open the curtains when the play started, pull it again for the intermission, pull it open for Act II, and then pull it a final time for the end of the play.

"Sure, Mr. Filmon!" We shook hands again.

Thus my volunteer career began.

The next day at 2:30, an announcement came over the P.A. during class. "Volunteers for the school play please make your way to the stage for rehearsal."

I jumped out of my seat, stuck my tongue out at Harry, and dashed down the hall.

When I arrived, the actors were milling about reading their lines, and Mr. Filmon was busy coaching them. He didn't notice me.

I proceeded to the corner of the stage to rehearse pulling ropes. I looked up at the curtains. They were very heavy, very thick, and very tall. I could hardly see the top of them where they disappeared into the shadows. I felt the ropes and pulled them a bit. Everything seemed to be working properly.

Now what? I wandered over to where the actors were repeating their lines. It was something about rats.

"They're in my cupboards! They're in my beer barrel! What can we do? We've tried everything! Cats, dogs, poisons, traps!"

Mr. Filmon saw me standing there. "Hey Ken, what are you doing here?"

"I came for rehearsal."

"Oh, this is just for the actors. You can go back to class."

So much for getting out early. I should have auditioned for a rat or something. Harry snickered when I slunk into my desk chair.

But a week later, it was time for a dress rehearsal, and I took my appointed post at stage left, holding onto the ropes. Mr. Filmon shouted, "Okay, Ken, curtain call!"

I pulled the ropes, and the curtain opened. The rats scurried around, the people screamed and cried, the piper danced and played his flute. Mr. Filmon shouted again: "Okay, Ken, close the curtains."

A few minutes later, I opened the curtains for Act II. More dancing and flutes, shouting and clapping, the Pied Piper says goodbye, and Mr. Filmon shouts, "Okay, Ken!"

And I pulled the ropes a fourth time.

Mr. Filmon thanked everyone, and we went home.

The next night was the real thing. A couple of hundred parents and families gathered in the auditorium to see our performance. I was nervous but ready. The lights went down, and I waited for my cue. Nothing came. Finally, I heard a whisper. And then a bunch of whispers. "Ken! Curtain!"

I pulled the ropes, the curtain opened, and the music began.

After what felt like an eternity, fatigue started to creep into my legs. I briefly considered finding a chair to rest, but the fear of missing my cue kept me rooted in the shadows, leaning against the corner of the stage. From my hiding spot, I observed the whirlwind of activity: rats scurrying, children running, and the distant sounds of shrieks and shouts filling the air.

As the piper concluded his haunting melody and the rats disappeared from the stage, a momentary pause settled in the theatre. I anxiously awaited my cue, straining my ears for any indication of what to do next. However, to my surprise, silence engulfed the auditorium. Convinced that Act I had reached its conclusion, I made a split-second decision and pulled the ropes, closing the heavy curtains.

The sound of applause erupted from the audience, initially filling me with a sense of pride. But that fleeting triumph quickly faded as a swarm of irate actors closed in on me, their whispers filled with frustration. Their accusatory glares pierced through me as they demanded an explanation for my premature curtain call.

Embarrassment surged within me, urging me to escape the scene. Without a second thought, I sprinted toward the nearest exit, desperate to vanish forever from their sight. But just as I thought I had evaded my predicament, Mr. Filmon's voice pierced through the chaos, calling out to me, "Ken! What happened?"

Breathless and consumed by shame, I turned to face him, my words stumbling out, "I... I thought Act I was over!"

In that moment, Mr. Filmon's gaze softened as he met my eyes. He seemed to grasp the mix of foolishness and remorse weighing me down. He chose not to reprimand or belittle me; instead, he offered a glimmer of redemption. "Listen, Ken, let's not dwell on it right now. We still need you for Act II. Can you come back?"

Relief flooded over me, washing away the burden of humiliation and igniting a renewed sense of purpose. With determination in my heart, I grasped the ropes once more, ready to fulfill my role in Act II. And as if by a stroke of fortune, a mischievous rat took it upon itself to provide the perfect cue for my final line in the play. The next night, as the curtains rose again, I delivered a flawless performance that left the audience in awe.

Looking back, I recognized the shared responsibility between Mr. Filmon and me for what transpired on that stage. He had failed to adequately prepare me, and I had neglected to seek guidance. Yet, to his credit, he didn't tear me down or extinguish my spirit. Instead, he extended a compassionate hand, granting me a second chance to make things right.

As the years passed, that unforgettable experience with the Pied Piper played a crucial role in shaping my volunteer journey. It taught me the importance of readiness and preparation. When I embarked on the next chapter of my volunteer work, I made a vow to equip myself with knowledge and dedication. This time, I took centre stage, captivating audiences with my commitment and expertise.

2. Campaign Promises

Student Council President 1967-1968 (age 18) Royal York Collegiate Institute, Etobicoke, Ontario

"You should run for President, Ken."

As I stood at my locker, preparing to leave school, I found myself surrounded by three captivating young women. They were my classmates at Royal York Collegiate, and they wanted me to become a candidate for the upcoming Student Council election.

"It'll be fun, Ken! We'll handle your entire campaign!"

Initially, the idea of getting involved in politics didn't appeal to me. With the snow melting and the blossoms emerging, I was eagerly anticipating the summer vacation. Student Council had never been on my radar, let alone the idea of becoming the president.

But there I was, flanked by three intelligent and attractive girls who were the envy of every guy in our grade. Perhaps this was an opportunity I shouldn't pass up. My ego received a jolt, and I couldn't help but betray a nervous smile. Encouraged by the girls and my best friend Vic, who was the current president, I decided to accept their invitation and run for President of the Student Council.

We needed a campaign strategy, something beyond just putting my name on a poster. As the girls began brainstorming, an idea struck me.

"Hey! How about Expo 67?"

They looked at me, perplexed. They had no clue what I was referring to.

"You know! The world's fair in Montreal!"

I happened to know about Expo 67 because my mother had recently visited it. She described it as an extraordinary event showcasing the latest innovations and technologies, with the theme of "Man and His World." It coincided with Canada's 100th anniversary and had attracted 50 million visitors. My mother saw it as a revolutionary and historic opportunity not to be missed.

"Mom said it was amazing and suggested I go. Why don't we turn it into a school trip?"

The girls exchanged glances, and their excitement surpassed that of upgraded lockers or a newly paved basketball court. Laughter and applause filled the air as we realized we had found our election strategy.

We started planning the trip, considering the number of buses we would need, the cost per student, the duration of the stay in Montreal, and the required chaperones and teachers. The more we delved into the details, the more our enthusiasm grew. Word spread throughout the halls, generating buzz and anticipation.

A few weeks later, a thousand students filled the auditorium to hear the election speeches.

After opening with a joke that elicited laughter from the audience, I dropped a bombshell. "Elect Ken Hoyle for Student Council President, and I will organize three busloads of Royal York students to visit Expo 67!"

The crowd erupted in applause, even though only a handful of them had any knowledge of Expo 67.

I won the election by a landslide.

The next day, I walked into Principal Curnoe's office with a newfound confidence. He shook my hand and congratulated me on my victory.

"Thanks, Mr. Curnoe," I said, taking a seat across from his desk. "We've done extensive planning for the trip. We anticipate needing three buses because we expect around 120 students to sign up. We think September would be an ideal time for the trip to Montreal."

Mr. Curnoe furrowed his brow and tilted his head. "Oh, well, no."

"No what?"

"Ken, I'm afraid there won't be a trip."

"No trip? What do you mean? I promised everyone that if they elected me, they would get a chance to see Expo 67. This is a once-in-a-lifetime opportunity! I can't let them down! I made a promise!"

He explained that he couldn't support sending 120 teenagers to Montreal.

"But I promised!" I repeated.

"I'm sorry, Ken," he said, shaking his head.

I was taken aback. Didn't he understand the importance of keeping promises?

"Fine, Mr. Curnoe. If you won't help me keep my campaign promise, I'll go directly to the Toronto Board of Education. I'm sure the school trustees will recognize that Expo 67 offers a unique educational experience for the students of Royal York Collegiate."

With rage coursing through my veins, I stormed out of the office, my face flushed with indignation as I pushed past the secretaries and into the Friday afternoon sunshine.

However, I didn't get the chance to contact the Board. The following Monday morning, my homeroom teacher approached me. "The Principal wants to see you in his office."

It turned out that Principal Curnoe had taken the weekend to contemplate my threat of involving higher authorities and consider the potential impact on his career if the trustees got involved. Perhaps he also reconsidered the educational benefits that could arise from such an experience. We agreed to meet again to plan the trip in more detail. After a few additional meetings to ensure student well-being and safety, he gave his approval, appointing volunteer parents and teacher chaperones.

In fact, we exceeded expectations. Instead of three buses, we managed to secure five! In the fall of 1967, I embarked on a truly unforgettable journey with over 200 of my fellow students to Montreal and Expo 67. What an experience it was!

As the President of the Student Council for the following school year, I discovered the brighter side of volunteering. It came with a touch of popularity and the satisfaction of a job well done. I even had the honour of receiving the Joseph Bulova Trophy for "The student who has individually made the most outstanding contribution to the school through scholarship, leadership, and service."

Above all, I learned the value of achieving a moral victory. Fueled by my determination to keep a promise, encouraged by my mother, and fueled by my youthful naivete, I stood firm in my convictions. Principal Curnoe seemed to realize that his negativity and fear couldn't compete with such unwavering passion.

This experience propelled my confidence to new heights. Emboldened, I mustered the courage to ask one of my lovely classmates out on a date, and she said yes. It was a splendid way to conclude my high school days!

Ken Hoyle

Ken Hoyle
President

Pam Mills
Vice-President

Hi Ken!!! You were a really great Pres. this year!! (Best Pres. of R.Y. since Vic!!) - with a great pair of feet, + 32.8 miles worth of blisters! Good luck at Guelph!!!! Best Wishes (Pam)

The Students' Council would like to extend its thanks to the student body for making the 1967-68 year a successful one. Special thanks should be given to our staff advisers, who were invaluable aids to the many projects of the Council.

With the instigation of Spring Elections the Students' Council was able to organize a trip for 213 students to Expo '67. The Bulletin Board in the cafeteria was put into use this year to cut down on the number of announcements. The school award system was revised putting more emphasis on the student who contributes to Royal York through his service to the school. Royal York's first Winter Carnival was held this year and was a great success.

"School Spirit" has definitely increased this year as indicated by the response to this year's United Appeal Campaign in which the students raised over four thousand dollars (one thousand dollars over its goal), by its interest in the Winter Carnival and by the best attendance at the Formal in many years.

It has been a good year Royal Yorkers, one in which we pledged our honour, love, and loyalty through Royal York C.I.

3. The art of quitting

House Advisor, University of Guelph, Ontario 1969-70 (age 20-21)

Quitting can be a valuable skill for volunteers. It allows you to prioritize your time and energy and avoid getting trapped in unproductive commitments. I learned the art of quitting during my time as a House Advisor at the University of Guelph.

As a house advisor, I mentored students, provided support, and ensured their well-being. Confidentiality was a core principle of the role, and I took it seriously. However, one incident shook my faith in the organization and its leadership.

During a training session, I overheard two advisors gossiping about a student's private information regarding her sexual orientation. This violated the confidentiality policy that we were all trained on. I was outraged and felt betrayed by the breach of trust.

Determined to address the issue, I sought out the programme director. However, he seemed disinterested and brushed off my concerns. His lack of action and response left me deeply disturbed. It was clear that the organization did not take confidentiality seriously, and I couldn't be associated with such disregard for ethics.

I believed that by remaining in the role, I would be compromising my integrity and reputation. So, despite the perks and the contractual commitment, I made the difficult decision to quit. It was a liberating choice that allowed me to maintain my principles, separate myself from the dishonorable actions of others, and preserve my own reputation.

Quitting taught me the power of taking a stand for what I believe in and refusing to compromise my values. It freed me from a toxic environment and paved the way for new opportunities and adventures. Quitting, in this case, was not a sign of failure, but rather a demonstration of strength and integrity.

By quitting the house advisor position, I regained control over my time and energy. Instead of feeling trapped in a role that no longer aligned with my values, I was able to pursue new endeavors that resonated with me.

The experience taught me a valuable lesson about the importance of quitting when necessary. It's not always easy to let go, especially when there are expectations or commitments involved. However, staying in a situation that compromises your integrity or fails to fulfill its promises can have long-lasting negative effects on your well-being.

Quitting is not a sign of weakness or failure; it is a strategic decision to protect yourself and maintain your principles. It requires courage and self-awareness to recognize when it's time to move on. By embracing the art of quitting, I discovered the power of self-advocacy and the ability to create positive change in my own life.

In the years that followed, I continued to apply this lesson in various aspects of my life. Whether it was volunteering for a cause that no longer resonated with me or leaving a job that stifled my growth, I became more attuned to my own needs and aspirations. Each time I quit, I opened doors to new opportunities and allowed myself to pursue endeavors that brought me fulfillment and joy.

So, to all those who fear quitting or see it as a negative act, I encourage you to reframe your perspective. Quitting can be a courageous and empowering choice. It's about taking control of your life, honoring your values, and creating space for new and meaningful experiences.

Remember, quitting is not the end—it's a stepping stone to a brighter future.

4. Luck on a bus

President, University of Guelph Ski Club, Ontario, 1970-71 (age 21-22)

Sometimes, life takes unexpected turns and luck plays a role in shaping our experiences. My involvement with the University of Guelph Ski Club not only allowed me to pursue my passion for skiing but also led me to meaningful connections and life-changing moments.

While training with the Canadian Olympic Downhill Ski Team, I encountered Heather, a woman who caught my attention. However, circumstances prevented us from getting acquainted at the time.

It was through the Ski Club and my role as president that our paths crossed again. But before that I had organized a ski trip to Quebec, I found myself seated next to a beautiful woman, not Heather on the bus—a fortunate turn of events that sparked a future connection between us.

The journey to Quebec was exciting and memorable. However, as luck would have it, the journey back home on the bus turned out to be a freezing ordeal. With no heat on the bus, we grew colder and colder until the driver sought help from a fire hall in Montreal. The firefighters kindly allowed us to park in their bay, providing warmth, blankets, and camaraderie. Eventually, we resumed our journey, only to face further heating issues, prompting a switch to another bus. Despite the challenges, we made it back to the university, exhausted but grateful.

When we arrived at the university the next morning, we must have looked like a sorry bunch. Sick and exhausted, we staggered to our rooms to recuperate.

A few days later, fresh and ready to go, I called on my travel companion to see how she was doing, hoping we could resume our newfound friendship. To my surprise, she acted standoffish. I guess it was only a ski-trip fling. As luck would have it, once I learned from others she was the daughter of a mafia boss, I felt a little less hurt.

Although my relationship with the woman from the ski trip didn't last, I soon turned my attention back to Heather. Her magnetic presence and shared interests, such as her passion for painting and the companionship of her pet duck, drew me closer to her. Through conversations, dinners and glasses of wine. I did not want a ski trip fling with her, I wanted something more lasting.

As good luck would have it, she said Yes and we celebrated our marriage in Montreal during the Christmas season of 1971, marking a significant milestone in our lives.

Life often unfolds in surprising ways, and it's important to embrace the twists and turns, acknowledging the role that luck can play. Through volunteering, pursuing our passions, and staying open to new connections, we allow ourselves to experience the richness and serendipity that life has to offer.

However, as the story of Heather and me in the context of the University of Guelph Ski Club comes to a close, a new chapter begins. In my subsequent volunteer experiences, I would have the opportunity to meet a diverse array of individuals, including a woman who would leave a lasting impression on me in a very different way.

5. Margaret the Bulldog

Chair, Certification Committee, Ontario Association of Landscape Architects (OALA),
Toronto, Ontario, 1979-1984 (age 30-35)

During my tenure as Chair of the Certification Committee at the Ontario Association of Landscape Architects (OALA) from 1979 to 1984, Margaret Scrivener, a Member of the Ontario Legislature, proved to be an instrumental figure in our quest for recognition and professional status. Margaret's sponsorship of the draft name act legislation, Bill PR37, helped shape the landscape architecture profession in Ontario and elevate its importance in urban planning.

Prior to the legislation, the term "landscape architect" held little meaning and could be used by anyone, even those with no relevant expertise. Our goal was to restrict the use of the title to OALA members and establish landscape architecture as a recognized profession. However, our efforts faced challenges and resistance for over a decade, and progress was slow.

In 1979, at the age of 30, I volunteered to become the Chair of the Certification Committee, sensing the weariness among senior members and the need for renewed efforts. Around the same time, the Ontario government published a report recommending improvements to the standards of existing professional organizations, which presented a perfect opportunity for us to push for recognition.

We set to work, improving our by-laws, enhancing governance oversight, and appointing respected figures within the landscape architecture community. However, to truly succeed, we needed a sponsor within the Ontario legislature who could champion our cause and present a private member's bill.

Enter Margaret Scrivener, a senior Member of Provincial Legislature (MPP) with the Conservative government. Margaret proved to be our bulldog, wasting no time in gaining the support of her fellow Conservative MPPs. When one of our initial supporters changed their stance, Margaret swiftly intervened and set things right. Her influence and clout were evident.

We hired a lawyer to help draft the legislation and negotiate with government lawyers. We engaged with Landscape Ontario, the landscape contractors' association, and secured their support. Meetings with government lawyers and MPPs followed, during which Margaret provided valuable guidance and advice.

At one point, Margaret even noticed that my brown suit was not suitable for the occasion and suggested I acquire a conservative blue suit to make a positive impression on the government officials. Wardrobe planning, it seemed, was a crucial factor in political lobbying.

We organized a dinner at the Sutton Hotel in Toronto to educate MPPs about landscape architecture and garner their support. While most Conservative members attended, none of the New Democratic Party members showed up, suspecting an attempt to buy their votes.

A close call came when a talk show host invited me to be a guest on his show to discuss our cause. Margaret advised against it, emphasizing the potential for controversy and opposition voices to deter MPPs from voting in our favor. We heeded her advice and kept a low profile, focusing on our goal without unnecessary attention.

After four years of hard work, we presented our proposed legislation to government lawyers, only to have it rejected. They offered a compromise that fell short of our expectations and needs. Margaret fiercely stood her ground, refusing to accept anything less than the exclusive right to use the name landscape architect.

Her persistence paid off. A few weeks later, on May 29, 1984, Bill PR37 received Royal Assent, granting us the exclusive right to use the title of landscape architect. We celebrated this significant achievement, and Margaret joined us in raising a glass to our success.

The impact of our efforts is felt today as landscape architects contribute to the planning and design of public spaces, creating enjoyable and sustainable environments for communities. Margaret's unwavering support and determination were pivotal in achieving our goal, and her role cannot be understated.

With the passing of Bill PR37, landscape architects in Ontario gained the exclusive right to use the title and solidified their professional status. It was a hard-won victory after 15 years of relentless effort and the dedication of many individuals, but Margaret Scrivener's unwavering support and tenacity stood out as a driving force behind our success.

Margaret's ability to navigate the political landscape and rally support among her Conservative colleagues was remarkable. She understood the importance of our cause and recognized the impact that landscape architects could have on shaping Ontario's cities, towns, and communities. Margaret's determination to secure the recognition and professional standing we sought was unmatched.

Beyond her role as our bulldog sponsor, Margaret provided invaluable guidance and advice throughout the process. She understood the intricacies of the political arena and knew when to push forward and when to tread carefully. When confronted with obstacles or potential setbacks, Margaret remained steadfast in her commitment and ensured that our objectives were not compromised.

Her influence extended not only to government officials but also within our own ranks. Margaret's insight into the importance of perception and presentation, such as suggesting a new suit for me, demonstrated her understanding of how to make a lasting impression and gain support for our cause.

Throughout our journey, Margaret's ability to advocate for landscape architects and navigate the complexities of the legislative process was truly exceptional. Her determination and unwavering commitment played a vital role in achieving our ultimate goal of professional recognition and the exclusive use of the title landscape architect.

Today, landscape architects in Ontario continue to shape and enhance the built environment, creating sustainable and functional spaces that improve the quality of life for residents and visitors alike. The impact of our professional designation and the recognition we received can be attributed in large part to the relentless efforts of Margaret Scrivener.

Her legacy as a champion for the landscape architecture profession in Ontario lives on, and her dedication and advocacy have left an indelible mark on the industry. Margaret's role as our bulldog sponsor will forever be remembered and appreciated as a driving force behind the success of landscape architects in Ontario.

6. Rotary Forest and Rotary Food

Chair, Environment Committee, Markham-Unionville Rotary Club, Markham, Ontario, 1989-1997 (age 40-48)

Planting trees is not as simple as it may seem, and it can be surprisingly expensive. That fact became evident when I revealed to the members of our local Rotary Club that it would cost $2,500 to plant just ten trees.

Amidst the gasps of the club members, Al Parker, the President, interjected, "Ten trees? Are you telling me it costs $250 for a single tree? You must be joking, right?"

I burst into laughter. It was actually Al who had encouraged me to propose this project to the members. As a Landscape Architect, I was well aware of tree prices, but it dawned on me that Al and the others had no clue.

"No, I'm not joking. Each tree weighs between 100 and 250 pounds and must be carefully transported from the nursery to its planting location."

Al responded, "But Ken, why are we purchasing such hefty trees? Why don't we just buy saplings for twenty-five dollars each? That way, we could plant a hundred trees instead of just ten."

"True, but if we opt for saplings, we would also need to water those trees every single week for a couple of years, or else we risk losing our investment."

All eyes were on me. They knew I was a Landscape Architect and that I knew what I was talking about. It was becoming apparent to them just how significant it was that Rotary International had initiated a program to plant one million trees worldwide by the year 2000, and equally significant that our local Rotary Club was contributing to this endeavor. It would require much more fundraising and effort than everyone had initially anticipated.

And so, in the Winter of 1990, under my guidance, the Markham-Unionville Rotary Club embarked on our tree-planting project. Our aim was to assist the Town of Markham in fulfilling an essential aspect of their park Master Plan — enriching biodiversity at the 305-acre Milne Dam Conservation Park. By strategically placing more trees at the park's entrance, we would create habitats for birds, toads, foxes, and other small animals, offering them protection from predators, including humans, as they moved from one grove to another.

To raise the necessary annual funds of $2,500 in time for the spring planting, we announced the Milne Park Tree-Planting Project to the public. As is customary in Rotary Clubs, fundraising often involves food. We manned our booth at the Markham Fall Fair, selling hamburgers, hot dogs, and sausages, and the funds began pouring in. Next, we launched our annual Christmas Ham Sales, which further bolstered our finances. During our weekly dinner meetings in December, I sported the infamous pig nose while announcing the results of our ham sales fundraising.

We scheduled our first event as close to International Earth Day as possible. On the designated day, our team gathered in the park early in the morning, enjoying coffee, croissants, and breakfast sandwiches. The local press covered the event, and we selected a small grove near the park entrance, taking advantage of the existing trees to provide shade and moisture for the new ones. We dug tree pits, carefully placed the trees in them, backfilled the pits with topsoil, and secured the trees with stakes.

It required a considerable amount of effort, but by early afternoon, we had completed the task. To celebrate and partake in the Rotary tradition of fellowship, we fired up the barbecue and enjoyed a satisfying lunch together.

Throughout the summer, the members of our Environment Committee diligently attended to the trees. Once a month, we weeded and watered them, followed by a barbecue and more fellowship. This regular ritual not only resulted in an impressively high success rate for the trees but also nurtured stronger bonds between the Rotary Club members.

> Adjacent to the "Sherwood Forest" area of Markham, a small but merry band of hooded "outlaws" were sighted redistributing nature's wealth in the form of a rich compost, in the Rotary Forest on Saturday morning. Begun in 1990, the Rotary Forest at Markham's Milne Park was designed to fast-track the naturalization of a portion of the Park.
>
> *Wheelmark* 2008 (Rotary newsletter)

As time went on, the grove we had planted became known as the Rotary Forest. Over the course of the next four years, while I continued to chair the Environment Committee, our Club managed to raise an additional $10,000. With these funds, we planted an additional 40 large-caliber trees, ensuring a wooded legacy for generations of humans and other creatures to come.

To be honest, this remarkable achievement would not have been possible without our weekly dinner meetings, hamburger booths, ham sales, and celebratory barbecues. It is one of the reasons why the Rotary Club remains so successful worldwide: the combination of fellowship and fundraising in the presence of delicious food and drink. It serves as a worthy model to be emulated by virtually every volunteer organization.

Our tree-planting project at Milne Dam Conservation Park left a lasting impact on both the natural landscape and the relationships within our Rotary Club. It serves as a testament to what a dedicated group of individuals can achieve when they work together towards a common goal.

7. Elephants on Main Street

Chair, Markham Village Music Festival, Markham, Ontario, 1994 (age 45)

Every year, during the Father's Day weekend in summer, Main Street in Markham Village is transformed into a grand stage for bands. Booths and food trucks replace cars, and thousands of people crowd the street to enjoy live music from various bands. It's a cherished tradition.

The festival was founded in 1978 to celebrate the charms of Markham Village, including its history, shops, restaurants, and craftspeople. Music was the perfect way to attract visitors and showcase the local community.

However, when I took over as Chair of the committee in 1994, the festival was facing challenges. Volunteer numbers were dwindling, and sponsorships from Main Street businesses were not being renewed. With only a few months left until Father's Day, we had no time to waste.

Like determined detectives, we went door-to-door, visiting every business on Main Street. However, we were met with grumbles and concerns from previously supportive businesses. Two common refrains emerged:

"How does the festival benefit my business?"

"The festival ends up costing me money."

Shop owners complained that festival-goers would browse their shops but not make purchases. Restaurants voiced concerns about food trucks diverting customers away from their establishments. Some expressed dissatisfaction with low-quality, foreign goods being sold at booths, overshadowing local craftsmanship.

Merchants shared their plans to shut down their shops for the festival weekend, which shocked me. I had believed that the festival was beneficial to local businesses. It was time to find a solution with the limited volunteer resources we had.

We decided to scale down the festival and relocate it to Morgan Park, just one block away from Main Street. This way, the shops could remain open, and we could reduce the number of food trucks to alleviate competition with local restaurants.

Once we announced the new plan, attitudes began to shift. Service clubs, churches, and new volunteers offered their assistance. Food trucks agreed to set up along the perimeter of the park, and Main Street restaurants reconsidered opening during the festival. Musicians and bands were willing to perform in the park.

On the day of the festival, the temperature soared to a scorching 35 degrees Celsius, making it the hottest festival in history. People moved slowly, seeking shade and relief from the blistering sun. As the day progressed, more and more attendees gathered in the park, eager to escape the heat.

Unexpectedly, we received reports of elephants on Main Street. Some local merchants, not involved with our committee, had organized their own street festival, unaware of the challenges that come with planning such an event. Chaos ensued, with vehicles jostling with pedestrians, and the elephants suffering from the hot pavement. Eventually, the street festival faltered, and people returned to Morgan Park.

After the festival, our committee and the Main Street Business Improvement Association held a debriefing. We made crucial decisions to bring the festival back to Main Street, with limitations on food trucks and higher standards for craft vendors. We encouraged Main Street businesses to embrace the festival and view it as an opportunity to engage potential customers.

Today, nearly 30 years after the elephant incident, the Markham Village Music Festival remains as strong as ever. With the exception of the pandemic years, the festival attracts up to 10,000 visitors to Main Street Markham, continuing the tradition that showcases the vibrant community spirit of the town.

8. The grit to say No

President, Old Markham Village Ratepayers Association, Markham, Ontario, 1995 to 1999 (age 46-50)

Are you currently a YES Volunteer or a NO Volunteer? I have experienced both roles in my volunteering journey.

During YES missions, you initiate projects, plant trees, organize trips, promote progress, and contribute to creating legislation.

During NO missions, your goal is to resist change, conserve beauty, and protect valued natural or built heritage. Both missions are valuable, but it's important to prioritize your mental and physical well-being.

Engaging in a NO mission can be challenging, as you often find yourself as a small group of part-time volunteers against a well-funded and powerful opposition. You may feel outnumbered and outflanked, like David challenging Goliath or standing alone as 20 logging trucks approach while you hug a tree.

When the final decision is made, your beloved tree, building, neighborhood, or organization might still be negatively impacted, and it can be heartbreaking. Before embarking on a NO mission, it's essential to acknowledge the odds. You are putting your heart and soul into something that may have only a slim chance of success. You must develop resilience for the limited time you dedicate to the cause and be prepared to accept the final outcome when the time comes.

I've preserved my well-being over the years by avoiding getting trapped in the Volunteer Vortex. This approach allows me to conserve energy for future missions. Just like the lyrics of Fred Astaire's song, I "pick myself up, dust myself off, and start all over again."

One NO mission stands out in my mind because it represents a typical situation in many North American cities. During the mid-1990s, wealthy developers, speculators, and frustrated drivers aimed to transform our beloved Main Street Markham Village in Ontario into another generic boulevard, sacrificing the essence of the entire Village. They desired faster traffic flow, prioritizing their movement elsewhere. They had the resources, time, and expertise to relentlessly pressure city hall, meet with civil servants and politicians, woo them with dinners, and promise political support.

Furthermore, the Province of Ontario offered the City $5 million to widen the street's south entrance to the Village, requiring the removal of trees and making it resemble other roads in the region.

In contrast, our Ratepayers Association lacked the same resources as our opponents. However, we believed that conserving Markham Village was of utmost importance, and we were determined to give it our all.

Why was widening the road problematic? Firstly, it increased traffic speed, making the downtown core less safe and less appealing for pedestrians. This diminished the quality of life for everyday activities like dining, socializing, shopping, entertainment, and housing. Secondly, increased traffic speed only provided temporary relief before congestion returned, contributing to more noise and pollution. This resulted in more frustrated drivers and reduced pedestrian safety. Thirdly, while constructing one lane of traffic required significant investment, it delivered no economic benefits to the neighborhood.

The northern end of the Village, Mount Joy, already suffered from the negative impacts of four lanes of traffic. Our suggestion was to reduce this section to two traveled lanes by converting the curb lanes into parking spaces, similar to the commercial core area of the Village. This approach would slow down traffic, protect pedestrians, move vehicles away from residences, and provide temporary parking for home occupation businesses.

Through traffic was eroding the Village's character, turning it into a mere thoroughfare. Our mission was to conserve it, and fortunately, existing laws supported our cause. In 1990, the Province designated the downtown as a Heritage Conservation District under the Ontario Heritage Act. However, the Ontario Ministry of Transportation contradicted the Province's heritage conservation efforts by offering financial support for road widening.

To address the pressure for road widening, Markham City initiated a planning study called Official Plan Amendment 108. Over the course of five years, our group dedicated ourselves to active engagement in the study. I chaired numerous association meetings, and together we made deputations to town staff and council, prepared reports, and spent countless hours at Council Chambers advocating for our cause.

It required tremendous sweat and hard work, but against all odds, our NO mission achieved success. We persuaded the City to decline the Province's $5 million offer to widen the road. We could conserve the Village, its southern entrance, and its historic residential area in the north. The trees in Vinegar Dip remained untouched, traffic moved at a slower pace, and we could focus on cherishing the beauty and enjoyment of our Village.

We celebrated this unlikely triumph! Today, when you visit Markham Village, you'll immediately notice that it remains a sought-after destination—an oasis amidst a regional desert, as described in James Howard Kunstler's 1993 book, "The Geography of Nowhere."

However, even though we won a single battle 25 years ago, the war is ongoing. The pressure from developers and drivers persists.

That's the reality of being a NO volunteer. You may achieve short-term victories, but the long-term success requires unwavering vigilance. You must be prepared to pick yourself up, re-energize, and pace yourself for the continuous challenges ahead. And if needed, pass the baton to the next dedicated volunteer who will carry on the mission.

9. Newfoundland hospitality

President, Canadian Society of Landscape Architects (CSLA), 1995-1996 (age 47)

My term as president of the CSLA was an unforgettable experience that allowed me to taste Canadian hospitality and admire the beauty of our country's landscape.

But before enjoying the perks, we had to get down to business. We embarked on a "resolution purge," reviewing and rescinding numerous unresolved resolutions from previous years. We focused on a few key items, such as assigning portfolios to board members and drafting a professional practice reciprocity agreement between provinces.

The primary mission during my presidency was to help all provincial landscape architect associations replicate the success of Ontario and B.C. in securing exclusive legislation for the landscape architect name. We aimed to support and encourage other Canadian associations to follow suit.

To achieve this goal, I became a national traveler, visiting cities and meeting with landscape architects from most provinces and the Northwest Territories. I related the path taken by the Ontario association to secure legislation, engaged with a diverse range of Canadians through my meetings, and conducted interviews with the press. Whenever possible, my colleagues accompanied me to showcase their cherished rural and urban landscapes.

During my travels, I experienced the beautiful trail system along the South Saskatchewan River in Saskatoon, explored the Forks in Winnipeg, and braved the winter landscape of Yellowknife. In Montreal, I brushed up on my French skills when visiting l'Association des Architectes Paysagistes du Québec (AAPQ). Despite my broken French during the speech, the audience appreciated it with thunderous applause.

It became apparent that many provincial associations faced challenges in terms of membership numbers, financial resources, and political influence required to achieve name act legislation. We recognized the need for extensive work ahead.

The highlight of my cross-country tour was Newfoundland. As the first CSLA president to visit the province, I was greeted with remarkable Newfoundland hospitality. Though not yet members of the Atlantic Provinces Association of Landscape Architects, the Newfoundland & Labrador Association actively promoted their profession with passion.

During my visit, they organized a grand reception, inviting landscape architects, architects, politicians, the press, and other professionals to meet me. It was an evening filled with engaging conversation, laughter, and the gift of a large framed photographic print of a polar bear on a Labrador rock outcrop. I was even screeched in as an honorary Newfie!

The following day, I participated in a CBC call-in show in St. John's, discussing landscape architecture and advocating for a school of landscape architecture in the Atlantic provinces. Landscape architects called in, asked questions, and dominated the show for an hour. Subsequently, Dalhousie University in Halifax, Nova Scotia began offering a degree in landscape architecture.

My hosts then took me to Cape St. Mary's Ecological Reserve, where I encountered thousands of living birds and saw a stuffed

Great Auk, an extinct species that humans wiped out by the 1850s.

After the whirlwind of activities, I found myself exhausted at the airport for my return trip to Ontario. Unfortunately, I fell asleep in the departure lounge and missed my flight, causing further delays.

When I finally arrived in Toronto at 2 am, the large framed polar bear photo awaited me in the room for oversized luggage.

As I reflect on my presidency and visit to Newfoundland, almost 27 years later, I cherish the memories of the people I met and the Canadian landscapes my colleagues shared with me. Volunteering can truly bring special rewards.

I remain hopeful that my presidency inspired associations in Alberta and Manitoba to pursue Name Act legislation for Landscape Architects, and I encourage others to follow suit in their respective provinces.

10. How to hoist a train station

Chair, Markham Village Conservancy, 1997-2001 (age 48-52)

"Intelligence," as Steven Pinker puts it, "is the ability to overcome obstacles in pursuit of a goal." According to the esteemed Harvard Professor of Cognitive Psychology, it was not just passion and determination that fueled our committee's efforts to save Markham's old train station—it was intelligence.

Considering the number and size of the obstacles we faced, we must have been remarkably intelligent, because we conquered them all and engineered a historic event in Markham's history.

The Markham Village Train Station had been standing since 1870, a good 15 years before the completion of the TransCanada Railway. It played a vital role in the town's growth, serving passengers, transporting freight, and even acting as a post office for the villagers.

Credit: Town of Markham

However, after more than a century of distinguished service, the station closed in the mid-1990s and fell into disrepair. The roof sagged, and the foundation looked precarious. In 1997, CN Rail, the owner, announced their intention to demolish the station due to liability concerns.

When Dianne More, a local public school teacher, heard about this, she rallied the community and called for a meeting. Having recently witnessed the demolition of an old feed mill, Dianne was determined to prevent the loss of yet another piece of her beloved hometown's history.

And so, the Save Our Station Committee (SOS) was born.

As a long time resident of Markham and a landscape architect practicing in the area, I was intrigued by the committee's passion. I volunteered to serve and was soon elected as the Chair. Over time, the committee evolved into the Markham Village Conservancy and became a registered charity.

My first task as Chair was to contact CN and request that they halt their pursuit of a demolition permit. To my surprise, they agreed not to pursue it as long as we continued our efforts towards the conservation of the station.

Obstacle #1 hurdled!

Next, we faced the challenge of public opinion. At the Markham Village Festival, our committee set up a booth with a prominent sign that read, "Save the Markham Train Station." Many passersby frowned, dismissed us with a "No thanks," or even shouted, "Tear it down! We don't want to spend our tax dollars on it."

Such negativity might have discouraged other committees, but not ours. We focused on the positive comments and kept our goal front and centre. We had a vivid vision of what the building could become, and with that vision, we pressed forward.

Obstacle #2 hurdled!

During the next four years, I had the pleasure of working with a dedicated mix of volunteers who played vital roles:

Paul Mingay, a local lawyer and descendant of one of Markham's pioneer families, helped us obtain charity status and provided ongoing advice.

Dorothea Moss, a researcher and historian, kept us fueled with food during our lengthy meetings.

Elizabeth Plashkes, a confident and articulate member, led our fundraising efforts. We applied for a $100,000 Millennial Grant from the Canadian government and later pursued a $100,000 loan from the Town of Markham. Remarkably, we received a $100,000 grant from the federal government, but the Town initially resisted providing the loan. However, with the intervention of Mayor Don Cousins and the Town's Chief Administrative Officer, we secured the loan. Now, we had $200,000.

Obstacle #3 hurdled!

However, one member of our committee was far from delightful. During meetings, he would snarl comments like, "What's the use? Do you really want to spend all this time and money?" His constant negativity dampened our collective enthusiasm. I confronted him after one meeting, suggesting that he might be better suited elsewhere.

We never saw him again. Removing that negative influence made a significant difference. By the next meeting, our morale skyrocketed, and it remained high throughout the rest of the project.

Obstacle #4 hurdled!

Each committee member took on specific roles and reported their progress at our monthly meetings. However, we soon encountered another major obstacle. Our architect, Philip Goldsmith, discovered that the original wood foundation was rotten when he consulted a structural engineer. To preserve the station, we needed to place it on a brand new concrete foundation.

"How on earth are we going to do that?" I asked.

"Pick it up and move it," was Philip's confident reply.

He completed the necessary drawings and estimated that restoring the station's structural soundness, adapting it for modern use, and enhancing its aesthetic would cost $750,000. We caught our breath and rolled up our sleeves once again, undeterred.

In addition to the federal government grant and the Town's loan, we sought corporate and private donations. We were also fortunate to receive a significant grant from GO Transit, Ontario's rapid transit system, which intended to use the station as one of their Markham stops—a dream come true.

Local developers and corporations, including Shell Canada, one of my clients, generously contributed to our cause. Shell, which operated a gas station across the street from the train station, was eager to be listed as a sponsor.

To raise additional funds, we commissioned a local artist to create a painting depicting the station in its heyday. We sold prints of the painting and auctioned off the original piece.

With sufficient funds in the bank, Philip put the project out for construction tender, and we hired a contractor within our budget.

I will never forget the day when, like an awestruck seven-year-old, I watched the entire building being hoisted onto steel rails and moved a hundred feet to the side. It was a heart-stopping moment for all of us.

Three weeks later, a new concrete foundation was cast on the original site, and the building was carefully placed back on top of it.

Obstacle #5 hurdled!

With a structurally sound foundation in place, the contractor proceeded with the renovations, transforming the station into a GO station with community gathering rooms.

A few months later, the Town of Markham received the Prince of Wales Municipal Heritage Leadership Award, becoming

Canada's first recipient for the conservation and adaptive reuse of a building.

The naysayers fell silent. CN Rail was ecstatic and sold the station to the Town of Markham for a mere dollar. GO Transit had a brand new station, and the Town of Markham conserved its oldest running train station while earning national recognition. To our surprise and relief, the Town also forgave us the $100,000 loan.

All of this was achieved because a group of 15 volunteers worked tirelessly for four years, utilizing their intelligence to overcome obstacles in pursuit of a goal. Many of us forged lifelong friendships along the way.

Today, the Markham Village Conservancy manages the station, renting out the community gathering rooms for private and public functions. The rental income helps maintain the station and generates funds for the Conservancy to undertake other community projects.

This achievement stands among the proudest moments of my volunteer career.

11. How to revive a dying tree

Chair, Ontario Urban Forest Council, 2000-2001 (age 51-52)

Today, the Ontario Urban Forest Council plays a vital role in tree-related decisions and initiatives across municipalities in Ontario. Comprised of experts from various fields such as arborists, foresters, landscape architects, planners, environmentalists, and more, the Council assists towns and cities in balancing urban development with the conservation and growth of green spaces. In fact, even in a bustling city like Toronto, there is a target to cover 30% of the land with tree canopy.

Given the strong environmental movement and the valuable insights provided by the members of the Ontario Urban Forest Council, municipalities increasingly recognize the benefits of trees in creating livable and sustainable cities. It was a remarkable honour when a colleague approached me, despite me not being a member at the time, and asked if I would volunteer as the Chair of the Council. Their confidence in my passion for conserving natural heritage in urban landscapes, combined with the knowledge that scientists were actively working on solutions for tree diseases, inspired me to accept the role.

However, as my colleague hurriedly departed for a new job in New Brunswick, he left me with a small box of file folders belonging to the Ontario Shade Tree Council. Little did I know what awaited me within those folders. A brief examination of the minutes and bank statements revealed a bleak reality. Dutch elm disease had not only decimated the elm trees but also the Council itself. Membership had plummeted from around 100 to a mere 10 individuals, with a paltry $200 remaining in the bank.

Gathering the remaining board members in my dining room, I candidly addressed the situation. "Folks, I have both bad news and good news. The bad news is that if this organization were an elm tree, we would have no choice but to cut it down." The previous board had been unwilling to take that difficult step, passing the responsibility onto us, the new board.

"The good news is that we still have $200 in the bank, which we can donate to the Conservation Council of Ontario. Here are the dissolution forms, already signed by me. Can I have a witness?"

Although my words were likely more nuanced and sensitive, the essence remained the same. I believed the organization was beyond saving. The five men sitting around the table appeared shocked and motionless, clutching their tea cups as if an arborist had just delivered news of their cherished tree's impending demise.

Then, one of them stood up. "No. No, we cannot allow this to happen."

The other members nodded in agreement, their eyes fixed on the table, contemplating the situation.

One board member slammed his fist on the table, releasing his grip on the tea cup. "No, we won't let this happen. We have to call Doug. He may not be aware of what's going on. He would never want this."

In the following moments, I witnessed a dying tree being resuscitated before my eyes. Chairs scraped against the floor, tea was hastily consumed, notes were exchanged, numbers were dialed, and heated conversations took place simultaneously. It turned out that this tree had far deeper roots than the records and bank statements indicated!

The following day, my phone rang incessantly. Founding members renewed their memberships and promised to attend the upcoming meeting. And attend they did. We rebranded the organization as the Ontario Urban Forest Council, embarked on a membership drive, and began designing a new logo.

My successor as Chair, Andy Kenny, an urban forester and professor at the University of Toronto, brought his passion and expertise to propel the OUFC to new heights of influence, a status it enjoys to this day.

Reflecting on the swift departure of the previous chair, I am filled with a mix of fascination and gratitude. Was he overwhelmed by the challenges? Did he lack a viable solution? Did he possess a solution but fear the potential reaction? Or perhaps he knew me well enough to trust that my naivety could revive a seemingly lifeless organization. Unfortunately, I never had the opportunity to ask him. Regardless of his motivations, I am profoundly grateful and proud. Despite the devastating impact of Dutch elm disease throughout the Province, it inadvertently contributed to the growth of a thriving organization with a diverse membership, dedicated to ensuring the continued health of the urban tree canopy.

12. Six parking spaces

Member, Little Red Barn Committee, Cambridge, Ontario, 2006 (age 57)

In Ontario, when a city proposes to erect a new development within a heritage conservation district or near a designated heritage building, they are usually required by law to engage the services of a professional heritage consultant. The Heritage Impact Assessment helps city planners conserve important features of old architecture, nurture continuity in the city's culture, and enhance each community's unique character.

Theoretically, at least.

In 2006, the Mayor of Cambridge and City Councillors wanted to build a brand new City Hall in one of the most iconic blocks in Galt village, right beside one of the oldest running farmers' markets in Canada and its historic city hall. The Heritage Impact Assessment was duly prepared.

However, the report completely ignored a third heritage building within meters of the site: an old livery stable known affectionately as the Little Red Barn.

It was the only surviving livery stable in Cambridge. Built circa 1880, it boasted relatively unique components, including a specially shaped brick known as Queen Closer, and an Ontario rare tier rafter system. Like many heritage buildings in Galt, it was constructed when horse barns were crafted with the same attention to detail as some of the West Galt mansions.

I was among a group of concerned citizens who sprang into action. We asked Council why the third heritage site was omitted from the report. Was it deliberately omitted to hasten the construction of the new city hall? Please don't tell us we are going to lose that lovely landmark, we pleaded.

The Mayor grunted and sighed. Several council members looked at their watches. One even rolled his eyes. Those pesky heritage people, they were thinking—trying to save the charming personality of our unique village on the Grand River. Let's humor them.

"Okay," said the Mayor. "Why don't you go ahead and produce a report. We'll look at it."

Rather than delaying the planning process, confronting the original heritage impact assessment consultants, and carefully assessing the barn's heritage value to the city, the City Council delegated their responsibility to a group of unpaid volunteers, offering little help from city staff and no funding.

And they gave us only one month.

We responded, "One month? That's not enough time."

"That's all you've got. All in favour?"

The Councillors all raised their hands. Anything to shoo those concerned citizens away and get our brand-spankin' new City Hall with corner offices and a big parking lot.

The Little Red Barn Conservation Committee was thus launched. As a landscape architect who helped conserve the old Markham Village Train Station, I volunteered to be a member. We rolled up our sleeves and got to work.

Since the City gave us no money, we raised funds amongst ourselves and hired a consultant, a structural engineer specializing in heritage structures, to assess the building's structural soundness. What his report revealed was that the stable was structurally sound and sitting within the perimeter of the planned City Hall parking lot.

We prepared newspaper articles speaking to the virtues of its conservation.

We made sure the barn fit the city's criteria for built heritage conservation.

We strategized many potential adaptive reuses for the space. It could be a Visitor Centre, City Heritage Office, Wedding Chapel, Bicycle Rental Centre, or a Coffee Shop.

We added that it would take up only six parking spaces in the designated parking lot. It would interfere with nothing else in the entire City Hall plan. Yet, it could deliver long-term benefits to the entire city.

We were excited about the prospect of saving this beautiful landmark. On the evening of the Council meeting one month later, our entire committee walked together towards the old city hall, ready to present our recommendations. As we turned the corner of Thorne Street, we stopped in our tracks.

Sitting right in front of the Little Red Barn, reflecting the orange rays of the setting sun, sat an excavator with a wrecking ball.

It felt like someone just kicked me in the gut.

They had no intention of listening to us or the findings of our report or following any of our recommendations. Nothing was going to stand in their way.

We shuffled into Council Chambers and presented our report and recommendations nonetheless. But as we did so, the Chief Administrative Officer smirked, Councillors chuckled, and the Mayor shook his head.

Of course, they voted against saving the barn. They believed six parking spaces offered more value to the people of Cambridge than a 120-year-old livery stable. The Little Red Barn was demolished the very next morning.

To this day, I cannot recall a more contemptuous and disrespectful act by a publicly elected body against its own citizens. The Council itself had appointed our volunteer committee to do a job, on our own time, at our own considerable expense. In return for our dedication and hard work, we were welcomed to the meeting by a flagrant display of disdain comprised of demolition equipment.

The experience was so traumatic that most people on our committee vowed never to volunteer again.

Not me. Not by a long shot.

13. What a difference a name makes

Chair, Canadian Association of Heritage Professionals, 2007-2008 (age 58-59)

As a volunteer with decades of experience, I've learned valuable lessons along the way. I've seen projects succeed and fail, experienced disappointment and heartbreak, and celebrated notable victories. These experiences have given me insights into the structure and weaknesses of volunteer organizations, and how a few changes can strengthen their position and effectiveness. Let me share an example of how I used this expertise to help an organization thrive.

When I took on the role of Chair for the Canadian Association of Heritage Professionals (CAHP) in 2007, I recognized that our profile as heritage professionals needed a boost, and our influence with Heritage Canada was limited. We had a weak presence among public servants at all levels of government, lacked active members from across the country, and our head office was located in Toronto instead of the nation's capital.

My mission as Chair was clear: to turn things around.

First, we addressed a significant issue with our organization's name. At the time, we were known as the Canadian Association of Professional Heritage Consultants, which excluded many professionals working in built and natural heritage conservation who were not independent consultants but government employees. We decided to change our name to the Canadian Association of Heritage Professionals. This simple shift instantly attracted public sector heritage professionals, and our membership doubled within a year.

Recognizing the importance of national representation, I noticed a gap in our organization's structure. We lacked formal representation from Quebec, a vital province in our national context. I reached out to members in Quebec and encouraged them to become directors. As a result, we gained representatives from every province and territory, transforming us into a truly national organization. To further strengthen our presence, we relocated our headquarters to Ottawa, the nation's capital.

With a solid foundation in place, we turned our attention to Heritage Canada, the federal ministry responsible for heritage conservation. We worked diligently to raise the profile of heritage professionals within the Canadian government and increase our influence in federal decision-making. Our efforts paid off as we became more influential in shaping heritage conservation policies and securing a larger budget for this important cause.

Today, the Canadian Association of Heritage Professionals boasts a membership of over 500 professionals from across the country. Through our collective efforts, historic buildings throughout Canada are being conserved and repurposed, avoiding unnecessary demolition. The work of our association has played a significant role in promoting the conservation and adaptation of old buildings, safeguarding our rich heritage for future generations.

14. Mad as hell and doomed to fail

Chair, Cambridge Civic League 2007-2011 (age 58-62)

The loss of the Little Red Barn hit me deeply, evoking a mix of intense sadness and seething anger. I knew that harbouring such anger would neither be healthy nor productive, so I decided to take action by starting a volunteer organization.

Chairing the Cambridge Civic League provided a more positive and civilized outlet for my emotions. We aimed to be a sophisticated entity composed of concerned citizens advocating for a noble mission. Our initial goals were clear: support members in presenting their positions to Cambridge Council, build member confidence in participating in the democratic process, reduce intimidation through education, and encourage members to run for election.

Our commitment to monitor City Council and prevent the repetition of demolitions like the Little Red Barn began to calm my boiling blood. At our first meeting, I observed defeated expressions and frustrated voices among the 20 people gathered in a circle behind my office. However, the shared expressions of disappointment and occasional outbursts felt cathartic. I believed that together we could make a difference.

Civic league wants dialogue with council

By Melissa Hancock
Times Staff

Communicating with Cambridge city council is difficult, according to Ken Hoyle, director of a local issues group. But former mayor Claudette Millar says more community members need to make an effort to engage in discussions about local issues.

"If we are going to have a successful city in the future...and be a contributing member of the (Waterloo) Region...we need dialogue," said Hoyle, director of the Cambridge Civic League.

Hoyle said there is a lack of dialogue in such areas as city growth and natural heritage conservation. Many issues brought up by council are "reactive" attempts to resolve problems, charged the director. More "proactive" approaches should be taken.

An erosion problem under the student housing project underway by University of Waterloo School of Architecture students will be a future "crisis" that the city will "react" to, predicted Hoyle, adding that he supports the housing project but not its location. He, who works as an urban designer, said he was "flabbergasted" by the decision to build the student house on the side of a hill.

Hoyle also said the location of the new civic administration building speaks to the lack of dialogue between council and the community.

The building should have been built along Hespeler Road near the YMCA, he said, and a "horrendous" parking situation could have been avoided. It could also have set "a new tone for architecture on Hespeler Road."

"It's one of the ugliest roads in the world," he charged. "We need to have open, consensus dialogue."

Which is why the Cambridge Civic League was formed. The Guelph Civic League, which formed in 2004, currently has about 15,000 members. Cambridge's group has about 14 members currently and can be joined by anyone who wants to openly discuss city issues.

"We have a great legacy here; how are we going to go into the future?" asked Hoyle.

The group meets periodically and newsletters are regularly sent to members via e-mail. Topics the group discusses include municipal elections and voting encouragement, economic development, planning and design, and the arts and culture.

"We don't have to settle for this level of government that we're getting," said the director, adding that he is not pro-amalgamation. "The region is imposing its will on this city."

However, getting people talking about issues that don't seem to directly affect them can be tricky, according to Millar, who sits on regional council as one of this city's representatives.

"When I was mayor I always felt it was a shame people (did not attend meetings regularly)," she maintained.

Community attendance, aside from delegations, is almost non-existent in council chambers week after week.

"I don't know how you resolve that," said the regional councillor.

The meeting agenda is available to download on the city's website – www.city.cambridge.on.ca – before each weekly meeting.

While Millar said she realizes not every resident owns a computer or has the Internet to look up meeting times and agendas, council and general committee meetings are held on alternating Monday nights at 7 p.m. in council chambers at 46 Dickson St. Meeting times or dates will differ during major holidays or summer months.

A citywide mail-out of all issues discussed or upcoming discussions would have a "horrendous" impact on city taxes, Millar noted, which could result in many unhappy residents. Meeting minutes are available online, too.

But some topics just don't seem to come up at council, maintained Hoyle, and more community workshops could be held.

Millar reminded that any issue a member of the public would like council to address can be mentioned – after signing in at the chambers that night – during a general committee meeting.

The length of time it takes for staff to address an issue during council depends on the complexity of the problem.

"I just don't know what more council could do," Millar conceded.

For more information about the Cambridge Civic League, send an e-mail to cambridge@yourcl.ca. The league's website is currently under construction.

To broaden our scope, we decided to address not only heritage buildings but also urban sprawl, roads, property taxes, sanitation, trails, traffic calming, neighborhood crime, and even city council salaries. We encouraged members to attend council meetings, and the overwhelming response demonstrated their motivation and engagement. We also set up a booth at the farmers' market, engaging citizens in discussions about local wards, candidates, and important election issues, while asserting our democratic right to participate in the election process, despite pushback from some councillors.

In the following months, we regularly met to discuss Council meeting outcomes and identify necessary actions. However, over time, our numbers dwindled, and fewer members attended meetings unless a specific issue interested them. Eventually, no one showed up, and I found myself sitting alone, gazing at my watch and out the window.

It became clear that my colleagues were giving up. Vigilance had worn them down. In hindsight, it became apparent that the League was doomed from the start, despite our best intentions.

Firstly, our organization's foundation was built on anger rather than a constructive approach. While we aspired to be a municipal watchdog, we often behaved like junkyard dogs, focusing on growling, biting, and venting our anger rather than actively participating in civic affairs.

Secondly, our initial goals were too lofty and lacked specificity. We failed to provide individualized support to members addressing their concerns with Council. Establishing clear boundaries, attainable objectives, and a single focus could have helped us sustain momentum. For instance, we could have exclusively focused on built heritage, committed to writing a monthly column for the local paper, or manned an educational booth at the Farmers Market.

Furthermore, the League faced significant funding limitations. Competing with fully salaried city staff, paid councillors, and well-funded developers proved challenging. Our ambitious mission relied heavily on the disposable free time of volunteers, which proved insufficient.

A lack of structure also hindered our progress. Merely meeting monthly to discuss Council proceedings was insufficient. We needed tangible actions and accomplishments, no matter how small, to keep members engaged.

Lastly, and perhaps most crucially, I failed to truly know my fellow volunteers. As Chair, I never took the time to connect with them on a personal level. Understanding their motivations, available time, skills, preferences, and dislikes could have helped assign tasks that aligned with their interests and empowered them to take ownership. Instead, individuals felt that their contributions were not valued, leading to a swift loss of motivation.

Despite these challenges, I remained committed to the cause for five long years, making it one of my most enduring volunteer commitments. Regrettably, the Cambridge Civic League achieved very little in relation to its stated and unstated goals, and it eventually became a burden rather than a source of fulfillment.

However, there was one positive outcome that emerged from the Cambridge Civic League. Some of our members, including Jan Liggett, who was one of the original members, went on to run for municipal council and was successfully elected. In fact, Jan is now the Mayor of Cambridge—a testament to the impact our organization had in fostering civic engagement and empowering individuals to take on leadership roles.

Reflecting on my experience with the League, I came to realize the importance of learning from our failures and understanding the necessary ingredients for a successful volunteer organization. It is essential to channel anger and frustration into constructive action, set realistic and specific goals, secure adequate funding and resources, establish clear structures and responsibilities, and most importantly, foster meaningful connections and empower volunteers based on their unique passions and skills.

While the Cambridge Civic League may not have achieved its intended objectives, it taught me invaluable lessons about the importance of strategic planning, effective communication, and building a strong foundation for volunteer initiatives. I carry these lessons with me as I continue to engage in volunteer work, ensuring that I create an environment where volunteers can thrive and make a meaningful impact in their communities.

Though my experience with the League was challenging and ultimately did not meet all of its goals, it served as a reminder of the complexity of civic engagement and the need for a holistic approach to effect change.

15. The joy of volunteering

Co-chair, Cambridge Municipal Heritage Advisory Committee, 2009 (age 60)

During my time volunteering with the Cambridge Municipal Heritage Advisory Committee (CMHAC), I experienced a stark contrast to my involvement with the Cambridge Civic League. While the League faced challenges and obstacles, the CMHAC achieved many of its goals and brought me immense personal satisfaction. This volunteer experience stands as one of my most cherished accomplishments.

The CMHAC was responsible for providing advice to the city council on heritage-related matters. According to the theory, owners of heritage buildings, including developers, were required to consult with our advisory committee before making changes to their buildings. However, I understood the uphill battle we faced, as evidenced by the Little Red Barn incident. The Committee's struggles exemplified why many people shy away from volunteering. Constantly battling apathy, witnessing the disregard for their advice by the city council, and encountering roadblocks can be discouraging, leading to burnout and resignation.

Nonetheless, in Cambridge, the Committee tirelessly worked to raise awareness about the importance of conserving built heritage and valued landscapes. We presented reports to the council, wrote articles in the local paper highlighting specific buildings, and aimed to facilitate positive change rather than hinder progress.

Unfortunately, some developers and realtors in Cambridge and the Region of Waterloo employed various tactics to destroy heritage structures obstructing their projects. They actively opposed heritage designation and argued against maintaining or expanding heritage conservation districts. Property owners of heritage buildings complained about restrictions instead of seeking guidance from heritage committees and applying for grants.

Furthermore, landscape conservation received little attention. Trees within heritage conservation districts were frequently removed without replacement. Beautiful landforms were desecrated, and rivers and streams were straightened and hardened with concrete or stone.

Nevertheless, I remained steadfast in my passion. After five years of dedication, I was honored to become the co-chair of the CMHAC. Instead of giving up, I made it worthwhile.

A significant factor contributing to the success and personal fulfillment I derived from the CMHAC was my collaboration with Valerie Spring, the Heritage Planner for the City of Cambridge. Valerie became our invaluable ally, providing a steady and reassuring presence during committee sessions where we deliberated on contentious matters and formulated recommendations. She was a consummate professional, deeply knowledgeable, and taught me invaluable lessons.

Here's where I made my volunteering truly worth it. As the proud owner of two heritage buildings—a designated office under the Ontario Heritage Act and our circa 1844 home—I leveraged Valerie's expertise to the fullest. I sought her guidance when I wanted to paint the office building, upgrade the exterior lighting, and replace the aging eavestroughs. Who better to consult than Valerie?

Valerie helped me select suitable paint colors and lighting fixtures that respected the historical context. She connected me with a skilled Mennonite contractor who could replicate the round tube eavestroughs typical of the 1840s. Furthermore, she assisted me in finding and completing grant applications from various levels of government. In the end, I secured $5,000 in funding, with a delightful coincidence of $2,500 coming from both the City of Cambridge and the Region of Waterloo.

The joy I experienced through volunteering was undeniable.

This rewarding experience with the CMHAC reinforced the importance of collaboration, expertise, and leveraging resources to achieve meaningful outcomes. It exemplified how volunteers and professionals working together can make a lasting impact on heritage conservation.

16. Leadership at its best

Chair, Grand River Film Festival, Cambridge, Ontario 2012-2014 (age 63-65)

In 2007, I felt the need to take a break from political engagement and built heritage conservation. Seeking something new and enjoyable, my wife and I decided to volunteer for our local film festival, the Grand River Film Festival (GRFF). We began by taking tickets at the door during the inaugural event, and despite the modest turnout, we were captivated by the experience after watching Guy Maddin's "My Winnipeg."

Like most festivals, the GRFF faced challenges in its early years as the board struggled to make decisions regarding film choices, venues, schedules, sponsors, and marketing. However, a serendipitous encounter led to a turning point. A board member, Bill Schwarz, impressed by an event at the Cambridge Centre for the Arts, approached Tamara Louks, the coordinator, with a proposition. He recognized the need for someone like her to bring organization and efficiency to the GRFF, which was suffering from a lack of progress due to egos and indecision. Luckily, Tamara agreed to take on the role and became the director, bringing practical project management skills and transforming the festival.

Under Tamara's creative leadership, we realized the need for a strategic plan and hired a consultant to guide us. Implementing the strategic plan and its associated initiatives turned the GRFF around and set it on a path to success. In 2012, after five years of volunteering at the door, I took on the role of Chair of the Board. Tamara quickly educated me on the intricacies of the festival, and together, we worked effectively to propel it forward.

Tamara's resourcefulness allowed us to attract celebrities to the festival. Through her connections, we arranged for Susan Sarandon, a close friend of a film director, to attend and serve as the narrator for a locally produced film called "The Entrepreneur" in 2012. We also showcased "The Creator's Game," produced by Candace Maracle from Six Nations of the Grand River, and organized a special viewing for Six Nations students with a Q&A session with Maracle. Additionally, we invited local celebrity boxer Fitz Vanderpool, "The Whip," to speak during the screening of "China Heavyweight." To elevate the festival's profile, we enlisted the services of a local journalist and photographer and hosted a grand party on the final night, inviting all the sponsors to attend.

In 2014, I stepped down as Chair, adhering to my belief that volunteers should rotate positions to maintain interest and keep the organization vibrant. I volunteered for fundraising, a new challenge for me. With guidance from Tamara, I reached out to existing sponsors to confirm their continued support and offered them additional benefits. I also approached local businesses we knew, such as my auto dealership, a real estate broker, and a restaurant, to invite them to become new sponsors.

To my surprise, all were receptive, and I found fulfillment in my fundraising success.

Cold calls to unfamiliar businesses proved to be more difficult. Despite encountering numerous excuses to avoid making these calls, I eventually mustered the courage to reach out, even if I fumbled for words. While not all of these calls resulted in new sponsorships, they set the stage for future seasons, which witnessed the festival's growing popularity.

The GRFF remains one of my most cherished volunteer memories. Thanks to Tamara's skilled leadership, a dedicated team of volunteers, and an efficient operational structure, the festival continues to embody its original passion and vision, even years after Tamara and I moved on to other endeavors. As a volunteer-led organization, the GRFF has now been delivering high-quality films to the Region of Waterloo for 15 years.

17. Fighting fires, fighting sabotage

Firefighter, Manager - Hedley Volunteer Fire Department
2018-2021 (age 69-72)

"You would think at age 69 it's time to hang up my skates and rest on my laurels.

Nope. I became a firefighter.

After retiring from my lifelong career as a Landscape Architect, my wife Karen and I sold our home and office in Cambridge and headed west to a tiny village four provinces away.

An old gold mining town in southern British Columbia, Hedley boasts a stunning natural environment. Though we rely upon upper levels of government for medical and emergency services and road maintenance, the community is proud of its self-sufficiency and resiliency. With few by-laws, it makes for unique homes and quirky people just like us. We are two of only 240 residents and love it.

Once a volunteer, always a volunteer. Why not join the Hedley Volunteer Fire Department?

Although now 69, I agreed to join the department to help the current manager who was approaching 80. They needed new blood. I liked like him and Chief McFarlane, who had served the department for 21 years, and was impressed by the dedication of the entire team. So, I agreed to become the new department manager. To be a good manager, it was important to me to also be a firefighter. I wanted to understand what it was all about. After 3 months of training, I qualified as a paid-on-call volunteer firefighter.

At 2:30 am on October 23, 2018, Karen and I were awakened by the village fire siren and a call from dispatch. We rushed to the bedroom window. It looked like the entire village was on fire. I ran to the firehall, donned my fire turnout gear, and headed to the heart of our village. It's historic restaurant, The Hitching Post was on fire.

The business owners who lived upstairs jumped out of the top story, permanently injuring themselves but escaping with their lives.

Our one and only fire truck, the pumper, was already there along with other team members fighting the flames consuming our 100-year-old restaurant. The incident commander assigned me to the front of the building.

Firehose in hand, I fought the blaze for four hours. The safety officer made sure I was hydrated, and the training instructor kept an eye on me.

"How are you doing, old man?"

"Okay!" I replied, with a chuckle.

Just before dawn, Karen arrived with peanut butter and jelly sandwiches for everyone. It was the best sandwich I had ever eaten. The women in town opened the Hedley Centre where firefighters took turns to rest and drink freshly-brewed coffee.

By 7:30 a.m., the fire was almost out. The Safety Officer noticed me shivering from the chill of the morning and told me to go home for a hot shower. I took her advice and returned 30 minutes later to help extinguish the blaze. By 8:30, only smoldering embers remained.

My leg muscles felt like I had run a marathon. It took me two days before I could walk without wobbling.

As the manager of the Hedley Fire Department, I helped direct several improvements. We began to hold monthly meetings and took detailed minutes. I delegated specific tasks to the officers, and each assigned task was followed up monthly until completed. I secured a $22,000 grant to replace outdated fire equipment and prepared a schedule of training for the entire year.

However, as I became more engaged, I began to notice that our local government and employer, the Hedley Improvement District (HID), did not seem to appreciate our hard work. Several firefighters had resigned after years of service, and I was starting to understand why. They could not get the least cooperation from the HID in resolving errors—even on something as small as their T-4 tax slips.

The HID 2019 Chair's Annual Report did not thank us for our work or recognize the accomplishments over the previous year. Instead, it publicly accused the department—and me by innuendo—of "insubordination, bullying, and harassment" without appropriate documentation and an opportunity to defend ourselves.

We could hardly believe it. The team's commitment was obvious, and many hours of our time were unpaid. We could be aroused at any time of the day or night and put ourselves in danger for others' safety. I volunteered 80% of my time as manager, and the other officers volunteered many hours over a month. We traveled regularly to pick up fire department supplies, using our own vehicles and paying for our own gas, to neighboring towns and cities two or more hours away.

The HID's trustees' behavior ranged from apathy to outright petulance. While claiming they cared about firefighter safety, they did little to address clearly dangerous situations.

One example demonstrates what we were up against.

A provincial highway runs through Hedley, so when we were attending to motor vehicle incidents, we often had to reroute or calm the highway traffic. On several occasions, we had to stand outside, at night, in the dark, holding STOP and SLOW signs. The danger became apparent when we had to lunge out of the way of oncoming cars who had not seen us in time.

We wrote a letter to the HID trustees asking them to help us alleviate the danger. The request was very simple: "Ask the Ministry of Transportation to install two new street lights."

We received no initial response. We followed up, leaving voice messages and emails. Still no response. Finally, after several weeks, we managed to confront the HID Chair. Although the HID was responsible for lighting, she said, "We don't do new lighting. Plus, they are too expensive."

"Two street lights? You don't need to install the pole. You just have to install the light on the existing poles."

"Mmm. Well, um, the drivers can already see you. You're wearing reflective vests."

We repeated our original request, stating that reflective vests were insufficient for the cars barreling through town at highway speeds.

"Mmm. I don't know."

It took several more weeks and several more photographs of the highway at night for her to realize how dark the highway was. She finally agreed to write a letter to the Ministry of Transportation and Fortis Electric, the provider of street lighting for Hedley and the provincial highway running through town.

The Ministry replied that recent incidents on the highway were a result of speed, not lighting. They only agreed to place directional signage at the bend in the road to help drivers see the sharp curve. Fortis Electric, to my knowledge, never replied to the HID's request for two additional lights on existing poles, and the HID refused to follow up with them. And that was that.

Our continued frustration led to the first-ever meeting between the fire department officers and our employer—the HID trustees—in early 2021. They agreed to action items such as painting the firehall bays, which had not been painted for over 20 years. Nothing has happened to this day.

A couple of weeks after the meeting, there was a backyard fire in town that contravened Hedley's fire permit by-law. The Chief and other firefighters, including me, attended the scene. The Chief instructed the residents to extinguish the fire because it endangered their own and adjacent dwellings.

We invited one of the HID trustees to come to the scene and support the fire department. But when he showed up, he told the residents, "The Chief works for me. I'm his boss. You don't have to put the fire out."

This was the last straw. I had been witnessing this sort of behavior for two years. I resigned from my positions as manager and firefighter.

The Hedley Volunteer Fire Department, once a proud and dedicated team, now struggles to keep up with the demand for service in our community. And the HID trustees continue to show little support or appreciation for the firefighters' efforts.

I hope that the department will find its way back to its former glory and that the community will recognize the value of their volunteer firefighters. They deserve better.

18. What "okay" really means

Director, Hedley Community Club, 2019-2020 (age 70-71)

As housing prices soar in larger cities, the allure of smaller communities with remote work opportunities becomes increasingly appealing. One such gem is Hedley, B.C., nestled amidst breathtaking mountains and the magnificent Similkameen River Valley. It offers an enticing option for those seeking a peaceful, picturesque village to call home. With reasonable real estate values, you can work remotely and raise a family in a place that is not only serene but also awe-inspiring.

What sets Hedley apart is its close-knit community. In this village, walking to and from the local grocery store allows you to quickly get to know your neighbors, who are mostly friendly and caring. It's the kind of place where everyone knows everyone, fostering a sense of camaraderie and belonging. You can even explore the town's rich mining history at the Hedley Museum while sipping tea and savoring a slice of delicious lemon meringue pie. Additionally, the Hedley Centre serves as a multifunctional space that accommodates social activities, dining, polling stations for provincial and federal elections, and even the local government's annual general meeting. Morning coffees, monthly pancake breakfasts, seasonal festive dinners, and exercise sessions are just some of the activities that bring the community together.

One highlight of the year is the annual summer dinner and street dance, organized by the Hedley Community Club. They close off the street, and with a $15 admission fee, they prepare a delightful dinner and hire a band to entertain the crowd. People from far and wide flock to Hedley, and by 9 pm, the streets are filled with a couple of hundred individuals of all ages, reveling in various stages of "happiness."

However, despite having a population of only 240 people, Hedley suffers from a lack of community volunteers and board members. This volunteer drought poses a significant challenge for the future of Hedley. Without dedicated volunteers, small local organizations struggle to thrive from one generation to the next. Recognizing this issue, my wife Karen and I decided to join the Hedley Community Club in 2018, attending monthly meetings and actively engaging in local activities.

Eager to make an impact, I wasted no time in suggesting an important initiative to the Club Board of Directors. Fresh in my role as a firefighter, I proposed a project called "Boulevard Boost" aimed at reducing the risk of wildfires by cleaning up Hedley's boulevards. The Board liked the idea, and with a small grant from FireSmart BC, we set to work. On Earth Day 2018, Karen, myself, and 13 other members of the club, fire department, and the community gathered 1,500 pounds of dry grasses from Hedley's boulevards. We loaded them onto a dump truck and transported them to a transfer station for composting. To show our appreciation, the Club hosted a barbeque for the hardworking volunteers. Boulevard Boost proved to be a resounding success and continues to this day.

Motivated by this achievement, I decided to take on a more significant role within the Club. In 2019, I ran for Director and was elected to the position. With a vision to enhance the village's infrastructure, I proposed the idea of a Trails Master Plan. Hedley deserved a dedicated trail for pedestrians and cyclists, connected to regional trails and integrated with parkettes and our beloved baseball diamond. The plan had the potential to secure funds from the Region for design and construction.

Drawing on my professional experience designing and managing the construction of trails, I presented three concepts for discussion. The response from people outside the Club was enthusiastic, and they showed immense support for the plan.

In early 2020, I stood before the Club meeting, seeking approval to move forward with the next steps, including gaining regional approval and exploring funding opportunities. However, to my astonishment, the previous chair of the Board dismissed the idea without even giving it a proper consideration. "We're not going to do any of this," he stated, citing reasons like insufficient manpower and time constraints. As I looked around the room, hoping for someone to challenge his viewpoint, all I encountered were diverted gazes, silently aligning with the individual who wanted to shut down the project.

I was taken aback, realizing that their initial "Okay" had been nothing more than empty words, meant to pacify rather than encourage action. It seemed that they never expected me to take their approval seriously and follow through with my plans. It became evident that in this Club, any long-term project involving structure, accountability, and adherence to timelines was nothing more than a pipe dream. The focus of the Club predominantly revolved around Monday night football, with plans, budgets, minutes, agendas, and elections deemed unnecessary and burdensome. The meetings were often poorly attended, and even the Chair frequently skipped them. With no new blood willing to serve on the Board, the existing Chair and Secretary held their positions uncontested for years.

While this may be acceptable for many community clubs, it presented a significant challenge for Hedley, considering our small population and limited resources. Given the success of Boulevard Boost and the vibrant Street Dance, I couldn't help but wonder why the Community Club couldn't serve as the ideal platform for succession planning and implementing small-scale infrastructure projects. Especially when there was a seasoned volunteer like myself on the Board, it appeared to be an opportunity too valuable to pass up.

However, they did pass up the opportunity, and ultimately, I made the difficult decision to resign from the Board. Although this experience left me disheartened, I refused to give up on serving my community. I knew there were other avenues through which I could make a difference.

19. The importance of a badge

Local Assistant to the B.C. Fire Commissioner, 2020-2021 (age 71-72)

In 2020, at the age of 71, I had the opportunity to volunteer as the Local Assistant to the B.C. Fire Commissioner through the Hedley Fire Department. This role involved recording the estimated value of fire-damaged structures and the resources utilized during firefighting efforts. While I wasn't responsible for determining the cause of the fires, I was granted access to private properties to assess the damage. To establish authority and facilitate access, the Fire Service Advisor offered me a badge, much like those worn or carried by law enforcement officers.

However, upon receiving the offer, I politely declined the badge. I didn't want my neighbors to perceive me as a law enforcement officer, as displaying authority through vehicles, uniforms, or badges wasn't important to me. The Advisor seemed surprised but eventually accepted my decision with a shrug.

Unbeknownst to me, this simple act of declining the badge had unintended consequences. In August 2020, a significant fire engulfed one residence and damaged two others. Although I was out of town at the time and didn't participate in fighting the fire, I interviewed property owners and firefighters to piece together the details of the event. I completed the necessary forms for all three properties and submitted them to the Fire Commissioner's office, fulfilling my obligations under the Fire Services Act.

I found great satisfaction in my role as the Local Assistant, but when I decided to step down from the fire department in the spring of 2021, I also resigned from the position. Upon submitting my resignation, the Advisor casually mentioned that I should return my badge. It was then that I reminded him that I had never accepted a badge in the first place.

To my surprise, this revelation seemed to have significant implications. It seemed that because I had declined the badge, the Fire Service Advisor had interpreted it as a refusal to accept fully the position of Local Assistant. Consequently, I had never officially held the title, even though I had fulfilled the duties and responsibilities associated with the role. In addition, when questioned about the need for new local assistant The Advisor's nonchalant response suggested that meeting the requirements of the Fire Services Act could be fulfilled by the local RCMP and it wasn't crucial for an improvement district like ours to have a local assistant.

As a result, to this day, there is still no Local Assistant appointed by our improvement district. Despite my dedication and the positive experience I had in the role, it seems that fulfilling the requirements of the Fire Services Act by the appointment of a Local Assistant to the Fire Commissioner is unimportant.

20. Village coup d'etat

Secretary, Hedley Centre, April-May 2022 (age 73)

In my quest to be of service to my new community in Hedley, I joined various organizations, including the Hedley Museum, Hedley Community Club, Hedley Centre, and the Fire Department. I quickly noticed that these organizations lacked structure and long-term planning, while my career motto "Look ahead and see the end form the beginning" emphasized looking ahead and planning for the future.

I initially volunteered for the Museum, offering plans to reconstruct its front steps and rebuild the aging wheelchair ramp. I also organized the regrading and seeding of the rear yard. However, when I asked for a supporting letter from the Museum to apply for a grant to improve the firehall grounds, they refused. Concerned about potential tax increases, they were unwilling to support improvements that would benefit both organizations. Consequently, I withdrew my volunteer support for the Museum.

Having already ceased my involvement with the Community Club and the Fire Department, I turned my attention to the Hedley Centre. I volunteered to help with various tasks, such as washing dishes during pancake breakfasts and serving coffee. Recognizing that the Centre's yard needed attention, I took it upon myself to repair the fence, cut the lawn, and water the planters. I also arranged for a new Canadian flag and facilitated the planting of three trees using a bequest from a former member.

In April, during the Centre's board meeting, it was revealed that no board member wanted to take on the role of secretary. I stepped forward and volunteered for the position, which was subsequently assigned to me. As the new secretary, I diligently prepared the minutes for the April and May meetings. During the May meeting, I suggested the creation of an operating manual to ensure continuity and serve as a reference guide for the Centre's future success. I offered to prepare a draft for this purpose.

However, in June, I was unable to attend the meeting and asked another director, Freda, to take the minutes on my behalf. To my surprise, I received the minutes only on the morning of the July meeting. It contained a lengthy concern that had not been discussed in June, suggesting that a reference guide would restrict the board's actions and diminish the organization's enjoyment. What startled me even more was the statement under New Business: "Search for a permanent secretary is ongoing."

Seeking clarification during the meeting, the director who took the minutes spoke up, stating that my position as secretary had always been temporary, and she now wanted to assume the role permanently. The other directors remained silent and avoided eye contact. It became evident that the board was not interested in long-term planning or being held accountable for tasks that would ensure the Centre's progress. Rather than waiting to discuss the draft guide in a future meeting, they opted to remove me as secretary immediately.

The board had formed a close-knit group of friends who prioritized fun and camaraderie over structure and strategic planning. They were effective in handling immediate matters and keeping the Centre operational but showed little interest in planning for the future. Their lack of enthusiasm for long-term viability led them to orchestrate my removal as secretary.

Realizing the board's intentions, I quickly transferred the secretary's responsibilities to the director who desired the position. I chose not to fight for the role and was glad that someone was stepping forward to fulfill an important board role.

Although my volunteer experiences at the Community Club, Fire Department, Museum, and Hedley Centre were not personally rewarding and relatively short-lived, I take satisfaction in having contributed to each organization's success helping to raise collectively close to $100,000 from external sources over five years for their and the community's benefit.

And my volunteer journey continues.

What a ride!

Despite the recent coup d'état, there are still ample opportunities for me to contribute and make a difference. One such role is serving as the chair of the Hedley/Upper Similkameen Indian Band FireSmart Community Board. Our primary objective is to mitigate the impact of wildfires on Hedley. With funding secured, we have organized annual community FireSmart seminars for the past three years, along with a defueling (chipper) event in spring 2022 and 2023.

Additionally, I continue to be actively involved in the Canadian Society of Landscape Architects, where I have recently reviewed their proposed Strategic Plan for 2023-2026.

I strongly believe in the power of volunteering. It not only enhances the economic vitality of a community but also fosters civic pride. Simple acts, such as maintaining well-kept planters in public spaces, can send a message that the community cares and is worth investing in, potentially influencing real estate purchases. Volunteer leadership can also contribute to the success of the private sector by generating the need to purchase their services and products via volunteer organization projects.

Volunteers come from diverse backgrounds, bringing a wealth of knowledge, wisdom, and enthusiasm to a community. They play a crucial role in helping communities adapt to new challenges over time.

The benefits of volunteering are reciprocal. Volunteers gain personal growth by engaging in different organizations and projects. They are exposed to new environments that stretch their comfort zones, leading to continuous learning, improved understanding, and fresh perspectives. Their increased value in the job market enhances their employment prospects.

However, it is concerning that many volunteer boards fail to recognize the importance of treating their volunteers well. Organizations suffer as volunteers become disenchanted and eventually quit. Consequently, these disillusioned volunteers may miss out on future opportunities with other organizations.

This waste of immense potential can be mitigated by boards, executive teams, and volunteers themselves. By implementing the tips and insights I share in the following pages, organizations can create a more positive and fulfilling volunteer experience. My hope is that these suggestions resonate with you and inspire positive change.

Ten tips for organizations

For six decades, I have not only devoted my time and energy to organizations as a volunteer, but I have also recruited, trained, and mentored volunteers. As a result, I have experienced both sides of volunteering, stumbling through mistakes and omissions and learning valuable lessons.

In particular, I have witnessed organizations undermine volunteer resources and even abuse volunteers, leading to both short-term and long-term structural impairment of the organization and its mission.

As an organization, you can avoid these pitfalls, optimize your volunteer resources, maximize your organization's successes, and progress from strength to strength over the decades. Many organizations know how to do this well. The United Way, community foundations, and universities did not achieve their current positions by accident. They have learned how to recruit, train, and reward their volunteers. You can follow their lead, and here's how:

1. Cherish and nurture your volunteers.

A volunteer is a gift to be nurtured and cherished. People come to your organization with a host of talents, knowledge, skills, motives, and passions. It's not your job to simply take what they have to give. It's your job to take what they are offering you and give back to them in equal measure.

There are many ways to "pay" volunteers. The primary ones are recognition, support, and appreciation. Another is the social aspect of belonging to a group. Find out what kinds of rewards each volunteer values and find a way to give it to them.

Share your knowledge and skills with them, and make sure your more seasoned volunteers do the same. People derive immense satisfaction from learning new things and acquiring new skills. Give them every opportunity to learn. Consider switching and rotating roles to keep interest up and provide new learning experiences.

2. Equip your volunteers to do their jobs.

Do not expect your volunteers to purchase or pay for supplies. Do not expect them to foot the gas bill for a three-hour drive. In fact, do not expect them to know what they need. That's your job. If a volunteer finds that they are giving more to your organization than they are receiving in return, they will lose interest.

3. Get to know each of your volunteers.

Spend time getting to know each of your volunteers one-on-one. Observe what they do and how they do it. If they appear bored, confused, or uncomfortable, they will not serve your organization well. Find out what they need, what they want to do, what they enjoy doing, and what they are good at doing. Then strategize how to get them into the most suitable position.

4. Help your volunteers manage their expectations.

Many, especially young people, are driven by ideals or indignation. If your project is battling against corporate or government monoliths, old or missing legislation, strong public opinion, or deep-rooted tradition, your volunteers could quickly become discouraged and frustrated when they see little progress. They might quit or, worse, undermine your organization. However, if they can adjust their definition of success, focus on manageable steps, pace themselves, and enjoy the benefits of spending time with other volunteers, they can find reasons to stay and contribute meaningfully to your success.

5. Carefully assess a project before taking it on.

Is your organization suited for a particular project? Do you have the expertise to address the project's challenges? Can you partner with a more qualified or experienced organization? Should another organization take the lead? Should a government agency be responsible for the project? These are questions to ask yourself before embarking on a project that may result in extreme disappointment for your volunteers and your organization. Refer to Story 12 about the Little Red Barn.

6. Ensure continuity.

You don't want your volunteers to simply leave once they are done. Ask them to mentor or train new volunteers and pass on their knowledge and skills. Good organizations have this continuity built-in: when a chair completes their term, they become a "past chair," essentially advising the new chair and board.

7. Be prepared to politely decline a volunteer.

Ensure that each volunteer's character aligns with your organization's values. In some cases, you may be aware of a person's questionable history with other organizations, where they may have caused trouble or proven difficult to manage. Be prepared to ask them to leave. It may be more costly to keep them than it's worth.

8. Know when to say, "Thanks, but we need a professional for that."

Some volunteers offer to do things out of eagerness, commitment, or a desire to make an impression. However, some tasks may be too complex, time-consuming, or dangerous. If they attempt to tackle such tasks, it could pose a serious financial risk to your organization. In these cases, it's best to hire a professional.

9. Hire an Executive Director and prepare a strategic plan.

For small and new organizations, it is advisable to hire an executive director as soon as possible. The executive director can provide continuity, consistent leadership, and engage with other local, provincial, and national volunteer organizations. Consider sharing an executive director among two or more organizations if funds are limited. A strategic plan is an important tool that provides vision, direction, and a workable blueprint for action.

10. Prepare an Organization Reference Guide.

A guide plays several important aspects of an organization. It outlines roles and responsibilities of the board and committee chairs and organization policies. It acts as a neutral, impersonal arbiter, providing volunteers with instructions on what to do, how to do it, and what not to do. It helps new recruits become acquainted with your organization's culture and integrate more easily. It serves as a reference to resolve disagreements and confusion. Additionally, it helps maintain continuity and enables succession planning. Invite your volunteers to help you keep the guide up to date, revise it, and make it more effective.

Ten tips for volunteers

Over the course of my volunteer career, I have managed to maintain equilibrium, avoiding burnout and staying energized for new opportunities and projects. Here's how I do it:

1. Put yourself first.

To avoid sacrificing your personal life, health, family, and career, prioritize yourself over the organization that needs your help. Make sure you are taking care of your own needs and well-being.

2. Find balance in your life.

Volunteering should be just one aspect of your life and should not consume all of your time. Focus on maintaining a balance between yourself, your health, social life, love life, family and friends, entertainment, recreation, work, and alone time. This balance will help you stay resilient even when a volunteering project doesn't meet its goals or requires a longer commitment.

3. Gain as much as you give.

Ensure that your volunteering experience is mutually beneficial. If you're volunteering solely because the organization needs help or no one else is willing to do it, you may end up feeling trapped in a negative cycle. Before agreeing to a volunteer role, make sure you gain something valuable from the experience, such as new skills, knowledge, social interactions, or personal satisfaction. Regardless of the project's success, make sure you find fulfillment in doing the job.

4. Be prepared to quit.

If you find yourself in a volunteer position where you are not being supported, appreciated, or properly equipped to do the job, consider leaving. Similarly, if the volunteer role demands too much effort and time, it may be better to pass the torch to someone else. Recognize when it's necessary to step back and reassess your involvement.

5. Take time to recharge.

Engage in activities that help you recharge and gain clarity. Spend time alone in a quiet natural environment, write down your thoughts, read widely to broaden your perspective, and minimize distractions like television and social media platforms. These moments of reflection will provide clarity, help you make better decisions about which projects to take on, find solutions to problems, and know when it's time to quit.

6. Never go it alone.

Avoid isolating yourself in your volunteer work. Seek support from at least one other person who shares your passion or goals. Make presentations with supporters present, involve multiple speakers to address different aspects of the issue, and remember that you don't have to carry the burden alone.

7. Don't let obstacles discourage you.

When faced with obstacles or objections, stay focused on your goal. Rise above the challenges and escalate your appeal to higher levels of decision-makers or government authorities if necessary. Remember the phrase "Nolitum illigitamus carborundum," which translates to "Don't let the bastards wear you down." Stay resilient in the face of opposition.

8. See the end from the beginning.

Be prepared to accept defeats along the way to win the overall war. If you find yourself constantly trying to convince others of your passion, they may start ignoring you or avoiding you. Accept that you cannot change everyone's perspective or gain universal support. Recognize that others may share your interest without taking action or providing support, and that is okay.

9. Be true to yourself, keep your word, and be honest.

Stick to the values my mother taught me: be yourself, keep your word, and tell the truth. These simple principles will guide you in your volunteer work and help maintain your integrity.

10. Consider an advisory role.

Once you have gained knowledge, skills, and experience through volunteering, consider mentoring other volunteers or taking on advisory roles. Share your expertise by participating in panels, evaluating grant applications, or writing a book. These activities allow you to give back in a different capacity and continue making a positive impact.

Remember, volunteering should enhance your life, not consume it entirely. By following these principles, you can maintain a healthy balance, avoid burnout, and continue making a meaningful difference in your community.

Acknowledgments

I would like to express my heartfelt gratitude to the following individuals who played a significant role in the creation of "Life and Legacy of a Volunteer":

Laurie Soper: My editor and a talented writer herself. Laurie's guidance, patience, and skillful editing transformed my stories into engaging and memorable narratives. Her sense of humor and positive attitude made the process enjoyable and fulfilling. Thank you, Laurie, for your invaluable contribution.

Tamara Louks: My Beta reader and a valuable supporter. Tamara's enthusiastic and prompt feedback throughout the two-year journey was honest, uplifting, and straightforward. I deeply appreciate your time, wisdom, kindness, and generosity.

Karen Cummings: My Alpha reader and life partner. Karen serves as a necessary counterbalance in my life. Her encouragement and reminders of the broader world beyond my writing endeavors keep me grounded. Karen's honest critiques and unwavering support have been instrumental in shaping my work. I am grateful for her presence in my life and the love we share.

To these remarkable individuals, thank you for your guidance, honesty, skills, patience, and caring. "Life and Legacy of a VOLUNTEER" would not have been possible without your contributions.

About The Author

Born in Hamilton, Ontario and raised in Etobicoke, a suburb of Toronto, Ken first volunteered in grade six so he could skip class. That memorable event led to over 60 years of volunteering.

Following his 43-year professional career as a landscape architect he is now retired and living in Hedley B.C. He spends his time reading, writing, gardening, volunteering and walking his dog Gemma daily beside Hedley Creek. When not in Hedley he can be found travelling the world with his wife Karen.

Facebook.com/authorKenHoyle

Manufactured by Amazon.ca
Bolton, ON

37903900R00057